Reaching for the Sun

DAN M. KHANNA

Copyright © 2020 Dan M. Khanna

All rights reserved.

ISBN: 978-0578-68200-6

DEDICATION

To our astronauts and cosmonauts

Who explore our universe to try to

Find answers to the mystery

Of who we are in this undulating universe

And how it began.

CONTENTS

The Emotional Warpath	1
Visions of the Future	2
The Misfits	3
The Glitter of Dust	4
The Fake Ornaments	5
Finding Oneself	6
Watching My Own Corpse	7
God Must Be Amused	8
The Journey Back	9
Nice to be Screwed Up	11
The Final Pieces	12
A Broken Life	13
The Lonely Bystander	14
There was a Dream	15
Family of One	16
Gazing at the Future	17
Exit Gracefully	18
Remembering Mother on Mother's Day	19
A Loser's Life	20
A Model of Mistakes	21
Why Was I Born?	22
Intelligent Nightmare	23
Fate's Version	24
Why Win?	25
The End is Far	26
Not Afraid of Death	27
Burning in Every Color	28
Dreams are Reality	29
Pattern to This Madness	30
Lost in Life	31
Lost in the Jungle	32
Empty Heart	33
The Hole	34
Stock of One's Life	36
For God's Experiment	37
Standing on an Island	39
Running Away from Myself	41

Conflict with Myself	42
Can't Find Myself	43
Can't Stand Myself	45
Life Without Life	46
An Uncertain Life	47
Born to Lose	48
End to End It All	49
Rock Relationship with God	50
Life is a Prison	52
A Reluctant Life	53
Light at the End of a Tunnel	55
On My Birthday	56
On an Island	57
The Animal in Us	58
If the World Were Not Round	60
I Saw my Life in a Dream	61
Culinary Sexuality	62
Finding Life	63
Crawling Out of a Shell	64
Dying with Dignity	65
My Obituary	66
The Scarlet Letter	67
There Comes a Time	68
The Emotional Volcano	69
Alone in the Wilderness	70
Alone in the Desert	71
The Last Throw of the Dice	73
The Circus of Life	75
The End is Near	76
The Final Performance	77
Human Hypocrisy	78
Born on the Wrong Side of the Track	79
The Dynamics of the Heart	80
My Life with Me	81
Nits and Pieces	82
The Broken Arrow	83
The Curse of Life	84
The Flickering Flame	85
The Puppet	86

No Life in Life	87
The Future is Ending	88
Building Monuments of Ashes	89
The Abandoned Apartment	90
The War Within	92
I am Just a Speck	93
The Wishing Well	94
Break the Shell	95
Let the Adventure Begin	97
Family of One (2)	98
The Curse of Love	99
A Painful Satire	100
My Life's Grocery List	101
I am Not Good for Myself	102
Pattern of Behavior	103
Wasted Brilliance	104

THE EMOTIONAL WARPATH

The storm
That rises within me
To take on
The devastation
That life has
Done to me
Gathering
Storm within the storm
With a ferocious rage
That would like
To swallow
Life itself
Life that has done nothing
Except raped and ravaged me
As I survive
In an unkindly and unfriendly world
All alone and lonely
Emotionally charged
Ready for battle
No matter
What the odds are
For fighting alone
Is noble
Against all odds
Into victory
Savoring the glory
At an enormous
Emotional cost
For life is there to live
And live I must
Through any challenge
Or gantlet thrown my way
I am
On an emotional warpath.

VISIONS OF THE FUTURE

My future is bright
I can see
The bright light in the sunset
As the golden rays of sun
Gradually submerge
Into blue ocean
Taking with it
All hopes and dreams
Of a great future
Now lie beneath the ocean
In cool tranquil waters
Alive with faith
But resting in peace
They still shine
They radiate with a glow
Of a future that wasn't here.

THE MISFITS

As I look around my world
I realize that I am a misfit
I don't see eye to eye
With anyone or anything
I look at strangers
Who see me but ignore me
My values, their values
On two different planets
My existence, their existence
On two different tracks
We stare at each other
Knowing that we will be together
But never the same
Trying to exist
But not really existing
It is just the way
Misfits.

THE GLITTER IN THE DUST

The golden glitter
That glows in the dust
Of life
In its final glory
Sending a message
That there is still
A life
That glitters in the dust
A life of hope and faith
For dust is nothing
Scattered remnants
Of dreams
That once erected
Monuments from sand
Castles from dust
That withstood
The test of time
Only to fade into oblivion
Gathering the remnants
That forge a unique band
To build a foundation
Upon which a massive structure
Dedicated to the glory of life
Forms a formidable
Monument that stares at the future
Taunting it to attack
For it knows it cannot be destroyed
For it came from dust
And dust it will remain
And glitter with hope
for all it can do
Is build upon itself
To continue the cycle
Of dust to dust.

THE FALSE ORNAMENTS

The false ornaments
Adorned by many
Tell a story
That people want to hide
The glitter of illumination
To hide the dark beneath
Pretending to be
What they are
Artificial beings
In a real world
Hoping to be admired
By shallow beings
Concealing their souls
To hide the dull
That lurks there
For that exposure
Will unmask them
For they are not real.

FINDING ONESELF

I am not there
I see myself
In scattered fragments
Collecting pieces
To make a whole
With missing pieces
As a broken statute
I get erected
With holes and fractures
But I am there
In spirit
As I patch myself
An imperfect human
In an imperfect world
Still alive
But still searching
I went on a quest
To find myself
That which I had lost
Years ago
In the jungle of life
A piece there
Now I search
Under the rocks
On treetops
The scattered moss
The decaying trees
I find a bit
I find a remnant
I touch a memory
I awaken a soul
I am there.

LAUGHING AT MY OWN CORPSE

As I look at my corpse
Waiting to be burnt
I admire
How young I look
I may have aged physically
But mentally I am young
Still dreaming of a life
That has eluded me all of my life
I may be dead
But I am still alive
Ready to be burnt
But not destroyed
For only God can do that
And God loves me
And will take me in due time
Not a corpse
But a complete human.

GOD MUST BE AMUSED

I was created
For the amusement of the gods
A toy they can play with
After they have had their fun
To break their monotony
Of doing good to people
Who may not deserve it
So they need a sidekick
To amuse themselves
And I am that person
Full of frailties
Lessons of mistakes
Prone to messing up things
So they watch me
As I stumble
And hurt myself
Then they pick me up
To see if I can stand on my own
To see e crumble again
They laugh
To see a smart person
Make a jerk of himself
The feast of the gods
They roared hysterically
To see me get up clumsily
As they threw banana skins at me
To step on and fall
But that is okay
For I feel that I was worth it
I served my purpose
Amused God.

THE JOURNEY BACK

I left a land
Of my masters
In the hope of finding
A village of my dreams
The journey was wild
The road treacherous
Occasionally great scenery
Loving strangers
Who pointed you in the right direction
I traveled far
A quest for peace
Where I can die
With contentment
Sleeping with the
Wisdom of the ages
But dreams
Elude me
I kept staring
At the vast ocean
Waiting for my ship to come
The moments
Turn into days
Days into months
Months into years
The eyes losing their glitter
As the waves
Just continue their rhythm
Deafening the senses
Telling me that
My journey is over
It was worth it
Even though I was stranded alone
I learned a lot
About myself, other people and life
Not all good, not all bad
Just like life itself

So I must turn back
Back to where I came from
Back to my roots
Back to the land of my ancestors
What will I find there
When I get there
Charged with strange faces
Who look familiar
But are not the same
But it is my home
Where I can rest my head
And fall into a deep sleep
Not have to wake again
In the dust of my home
The land of my parents.

NICE TO BE SCREWED UP

I know I am screwed up
Otherwise why would I be in this mess
Lost relationships
Mediocre career, and
Struggling life
But then
It is not bad
To be screwed up
It can be quite beneficial
For it kills all expectations
You know
That anything you do
Will turn out to be a disaster
So why try
Just expect that life will go on
And you will be nothing
Just a forgotten human
It is nice to be screwed up.

THE FINAL PIECES

As I search for the final pieces
To put together
The last picture
That I have of me
A rocked landscape
Of ugly beauty
But it is still my picture
That tells its own story
Of joy and sorrow
It is a real picture
All I need to do
Is find the pieces
The final pieces
That is all
That is left of me
A few fragments.

A BROKEN LIFE

Life is a myriad of pieces
Put together to create a scene
That exacerbates its unique beauty
It is fragile
It is delicate
Prone to temptations
Held together by invisible strings
That may come apart
At any time
To scatter the pieces
In the jungle of humanity
As one gathers the pieces
To form a picture
That was once a reality
Now it is just
Broken pieces
Trying to fit together.

THE LONELY BYSTANDER

I am standing
At the shores of time
Watching the world go by
A world of strangers
Waving and gazing at nothing
Just an emptiness
Of humanity
The hollow souls
Living day to day
To be battered by the future
I am glad that I am not part of it
I see it but don't want to participate in it
For it is not my kind of world
Not my kind of people
So I remain a bystander
Staring at the images
A lonely bystander.

THERE WAS A DREAM

Contrary to what
The world may think
I had a dream
That I hoped to realize
During my lifetime
But life passed me by
And I kept
Staring at the dream
As it streamed past me
Not even letting me touch it
Just a fleeting illusion
Of a vision
That once as a dream
Now just
A figment of my imagination
A dream
That should have been a reality.

FAMILY OF ONE

I was alone
Before I was born
And then I had a family
A lovely family
That showered me with love
And sent me out
To conquer the world
Of my dreams
My family grew
I had my own family
And then my family
Started to disappear and dissipate
From many become few
And as people move on with their families
You are left alone
Just, a family of one.

GAZING AT THE FUTURE

As I look into my future
I see an emptiness
With scattered clouds
Hiding the abyss
That awaits me
As I journey toward it
Hovering lower
What will I find?
A mountain or a canyon
An ocean or a storm
But it is my future
That awaits me
Welcoming me with an embrace
Swallowing me into a new world
That is my future
And then that future
Is the present
It is now.

EXIT GRACEFULLY

As I stare at the sunset
The golden rays of
A drowning sun
Brighten the world
Temporarily
As it sinks
Into the calm bosom
Of the mysterious ocean
I wonder
How my exit from this world
Can be graceful and beautiful
Leaving an image
That will be a legacy
But that is just a dream
For I am an ordinary person
Who had dreams and visions
That all came crashing down
Through mistakes and misfortunes
As I await my time
To slip through the eternal gates
Unseen and unknown
A quiet end?
A turbulent end?
Finally, at peace
As golden rays
Engulf me
Welcoming me
For what I am
In the final sunset
With grace and beauty
A great end.

REMEMBERING MOTHER ON MOTHER'S DAY

There is still time
For Mother's Day
But that does not mean
That I cannot remember
My mother any other day
Actually, every day of my life
Is Mother's Day for me
I miss her every day
Though she has
Passed away to a better world
I know and I feel
That she watches over me
As I enter the sunset of my life
I am still her child
I still long to hug her
Hold her
And let my head rest in her lap
As she soothes my pain away
I long for her advice and counsel
For my mother
Knew me and believed in me
I was her
Creation of love
And undying faith
For she would have
Stopped me from hurting myself
In this perilous journey of life
I need her even more now
As I am alone
Trying to stand up to life
But, in my heart, I know
She is beside me
Holding me quietly
With overflowing love always.

A LOSER'S LIFE

A loser's life
Is a wonderful life
For it is devoid of expectations
Dreams have been squashed
And nothing great
To look for
It is a great life
For you know
Whatever you do
Will turn out wrong
Whether in career or relationship
So why try?
Just accept the inevitable
You came, you tried, you lost
Just accept it as part of fate
Destiny was not with you
And you were
Destined to be a loser.

A MODEL OF MISTAKES

I am a perfect model
Of a person
Who has mastered
The act of making mistakes
Whether in career or relationships
I do it with mastery
I have perfected the act
Squandering opportunities
Shunning the world
Inflicting wounds on myself
That have scarred my mind and body
Entombing me
In a shroud of mistakes
As I head towards
An ocean of oblivion
To be forgotten forever
Wiped from the face of this earth.

WHY WAS I BORN?

The reasons for my existence
Baffle me
And remain a mystery
Why was I born?
I serve nearly no purpose
In this life
Didn't matter
Accomplished nothing much
Just existed
As a mediocre
Whose life's end
Will not have
An obituary
Just a forgotten
Human like many
Nothing to show, so
Why was I born?

INTELLIGENT NIGHTMARE

The nightmares of life
Remind us
That we carry
Many hidden demons
In our minds
That occasionally crawl out
To haunt us
Scare us
And maybe tell us something
About ourselves
That we are not ready
To hear
Nightmares
Can be quite intelligent
They lay
Deep beneath our hearts
Forming images
To convey messages
That what we see
Is it real
There is a deep reality
That lives within us
That we are not explaining
We are losing our touch
Within ourselves
So nightmares are formed
To scare us
To remind us
That nightmares are the real truth
Seek inside us
Don't be scared
We are just dramatizing
Our inner souls
Trust us, we are intelligent.

FATE'S VERSION

My fate's version
Of my life
Is very different
Than my version
Of my life
The two travel
Parallel tracks
Dreams staring at dreams
Sharing a track
But not touching
I move in one direction
Fate pushes me in another
The hopes ad wishes
Just get squandered
By Fate's vision
And life goes on
In two different direction

WHY WIN?

Winning is everything.
But, why win at all?
Winning is glorified.
Actually, it can be quite depressing.
First, one has to work hard
To win
That takes time away
From fun
Then you have to compete
Against able and decent people
Whose dreams
May be more valuable than yours.
Why hurt them?
Then if you lose
That hurts
You will get false sympathy
From gloating people
Who are delighted
That you lost.
You feel depressed.
Should you try again?
Even, if you win
Now, you have to live up
To your new standard.
People look up to you
Waiting for you to stumble.
The pressure is building.
It is too much hard work.
The risks are many.
The rewards fleeting.
So why try?
Why win?

THE END IS FAR

I can see the end
Of my turbulent life
I reach out
To touch it
But it remains far
I want to draw close
But it escapes my grasp
I stumble, I fall
I crawl
But the end remains far
Reminding me
That my time
Is not yet over
I must wait my time
And still pay
For all my mistakes
As I get flogged
By life
As I move
Towards the end
Constantly reminding me
That the end is far.

NOT AFRAID OF DEATH

I stare at the face of death
And boldly ask,
What is the matter with you?
Are you afraid of me?
I am ready for you
Actually, I was ready
The day I was born
For, isn't birth
A journey towards death
So here I am
But you can't touch me yet
I still have dreams left
I still have unfinished business
I still have responsibilities to take care of
I still have unfinished ambitions
My time here on earth
Is not over yet
So you can't take me
You have to wait
For, I am not afraid of you.

BURNING IN EVERY COLOR

The flame
That illuminates
The world
Eventually extinguishes
But, in its lovely life
It burns in every color
Gold, yellow, orange, crimson, blue
It wants to fuel
Every feeling
Every thrill
As it nears its end
To be extinguished forever
But it wants to leave its mark
A final spark
That says
I have lived and burnt
Brightened and gave light
But as I flicker in the final burst
I want to glow in every color
A glorious end.

DREAMS ARE REALITY

We all have dreams
Dreams of a life
That we would like to have
Drams that ponder our minds
When we are asleep
Sending messages
From our unconscious
We need to merge our dreams
Real and unreal
For that is all we have
Bringing reality to our thoughts
Dreams are just manifestations
Of the lives
We live
All our life is a dream
Whether we are awake or asleep
In one sense
They are the same
Our dreams
Are our only reality
It is our lives.

PATTERN TO THIS MADNESS

We are all mad
Some time and some place
We do crazy things
Temporary insanity engulfs us
We hurt others
We hurt ourselves
As we try to find
A cure for our madness
That occasionally
Creeps up on us
There is a pattern
To this madness
It comes and goes
Depending on our emotional states
Our life experiences
Our contact with friends and family
Life and living
Shapes us
As we learn
To accept it
And live with it.

LOST IN LIFE

Somewhere
Along the way
Of my insignificant life
I lost my way
I did not start
In the right direction
But then I encountered
A turbulence
That led me astray
I chose directions
That led me nowhere
I retraced my steps
To start again
But wherever I went
Was a strange place
I was with people
But I was alone
Asking directions
Relying on my instincts
Still searching
For my true path
As I remain
Lost in life.

LOVE IN THE JUNGLE

The jungle of life
Is full of strange species
Some wild, some tame
Some friendly, some ferocious
Strange terrain
Unknown wildlife
I stand alone
In the middle
Surrounded by strange species
Unknown plants and vines
What to touch
What to avoid
What to eat
The temptations of life
Building on survival instincts
Wants to endure
The gentleness of wildlife
As I work my way
Through the jungle
Seeking another civilization
With its own wildness
As I travel
From jungle to jungle.

EMPTY HEART

I had a heart
That was full of love
Searching for meaning
In a meaningless world
It can hurt
It got trampled
It lost its wisdom
Became impulsive and irrational
Making mistakes
Until it lost its patience
And emptied itself
Creating a void
That shall forever
Remain empty
Never to hope
Never to dream
To avoid pain
Just flutter
An empty heart.

THE HOLE

The hole is dug
I dug it myself
With my bare hands
Clearing mud
As I crawled into it
I was proud
I wanted to create
The deepest hole
Without any help
I did it
I wanted to see
How deep it was
So I jumped in it
It was deep
It was dark
I was proud
Of my achievement
Until it dawned on me
How will I
Get out of it?
I can see
The light
At the top
Telling me
That my reach
Is not enough
Soon darkness
Will prevail
It will be dark
No light, no hope
Just earth
As it surrounds me
While I wait
For the inevitable
As I forever
Merge with the earth

To find a place
Of my own
In a hole
That I dug
Myself
For myself.

THE STOCK OF ONE'S LIFE

Where do I begin
How do I take
A stock of one's life
When there are
So many pluses and minuses
Good and bad
As I stand in the balance
Where will it tilt
I did good
I did wrong
Who am I to judge?
Can I be fair?
Can I be objective?
As I take
A stock of my life
I realize
It was a mediocre life
Just survival and struggle
Through occasional brilliance
But mostly mistakes and misjudgments
An uneventful life
That is my stock
Of my life

FOR GOD'S EXPERIMENT

As the twilight of life
Sets my sunset
I ponder
At my purpose
In the life
I lived and loved
I came alone
I will die alone
So what did I do
In the interim?
What did I accomplish?
Nothing much
Just a mediocre life
When I die
I will not even be missed
But just a few
For a short time
Until my memories
Fade into oblivion
And life goes on
So why did I come
To the Earth?
For God's amusement
As God sees
A decent, honest person
Struggle to survive
While evil flourishes all around
For giving me
The ability to love
But, not the satisfaction of love
Giving me great parents
But not their lifelong companionship
I am an experiment
For God to see
What an ordinary
Human creation
Goes through

As he struggles
To carve
A decent living
And deal with
All of the onslaught
Of the society
As the body takes
Punishment
Pummeled by every kind of illness
Gradually decaying
To test the human spirit
Yes, I am an
Experiment for God's amusement
So God can create
A perfect being
In His image.

STANDING ON AN ISLAND

I am standing
On a small island
Alone and uninhabited
All I see
Is the blue ocean
Surrounding me
No land in sight
I can't even tell
What is North
Where is West
Every direction
Just a vision
Of a land
That eludes me
I wait, I think
Should I try
To swim
But to where?
Or should
I wait
For a passing ship
But I wait
Many years
With no sightings
Or should I accept my fate
That I am stranded alone
And I will remain alone
On this
Desolate island
And spend
My remaining days
Surviving on the
Meager offerings of the island
As I learn
To accept the days and nights
That just keep passing by me
Still dreaming of a paradise
That was once within my grasp

But now as I close my eyes
To dream of land
Friends and lovers
With the ocean
Smashing on the beach
That is my paradise.

RUNNING AWAY FROM MYSELF

Some time ago
I left me
Ad ran away from myself
I wanted to be alone
Alone without me
So I can do
Whatever I wanted
Reckless and impulsive
Avoiding my inner voice
That would always
Tell me the trust
About myself
And my actions
But I did not
Want to hear it
For I thought
I had all the answers
I am me
I know it all
I can do what I want
Soon, our distance
Anew, so much
That we stopped
Talking
I continued
To make mistake after mistake
Until I lost confidence in me
And started
My search for myself
Trying to find
My inner voice
That would
Set me straight
And put me
On the right path
Full of promise
And peace
While I stop running away from myself.

CONFLICT WITH MYSELF

I am in a perpetual
Argument with myself
About the direction
Of my life
What I should do
I don't do
What I want to do
I don't do
I argue with myself
I justify my actions
Even though
They are self-hurting
I pursue a path
Of self-destruction
Just because
I fail to recognize
Myself
In the veil of conflict
That I cannot win
I will not win
As long as
I am in conflict
With myself.

CAN'T FIND MYSELF

I was told
To take a road
That is unknown and daunting
It was a promising start
To a potentially adventurous journey
I saw strange places
Experience the unknown
The road led me through
Forests and rivers
Hills and valleys
Beautiful scenery
Painful sights
But, somewhere
Along the way
I was alone
All alone
I had lost myself
I looked around
I reached out
But I could not
Find myself
I started to wonder
Where I lost me
In the jungle
On the banks of the river
Or the shores of the sea
Or atop the mountain
Of the depths of the valley
All of a sudden, I realized
I was alone
All directions seemed the same
Should I retrace my steps
To find myself
Or continue forward
Alone
Hoping that I may
Catch myself
Somewhere, some place

I stand still
Silent and quiet
Hoping to hear me
But the deadly silence
I cold
I shiver
The wilderness
Is weeing for me
I have to escape
To find myself
That I lost
Somewhere along the way
Without me
I am just a body
A carcass
That plods along
To die a wasteful death
But I can't let it happen
I have to find myself
And be one with me
A complete person
Full of hope and dreams
Just as when
I started my travels.

CAN'T STAND MYSELF

I look in the mirror
I see a face
It is not my face
It resembles me
But it has turned hideous
From the blows of life
Battered and scarred
Wrinkles creased with blood
Infected by
Friends and foes
It is not my face
But it is
I can't stand
To look at it
What have I become
A monster
That is devouring myself
I reach out
To touch the face
It escapes my grasp
And smiles unchangingly
As I see my image
Sneer at me
And tell me
What I have done to myself
Around baby face
Turned into
The face of Frankenstein's monster
I did it
Life did
Does it matter?
I am not me anymore
Just a remnant
Of a dream
That once I had
I am no longer me
Just a remnant
Of a lost soul.

LIFE WITHOUT LIFE

I live life
Without life
I breathe
I eat
I sleep
But there is no life
In my life
Just motions
Of routine existence
I claw my way
To world's delayed end
Where I can rest
In pure
And find life
That should have been
Mine
A life
With life.

AN UNCERTAIN LIFE

I could never
Really grasp my life
Every time I tried to embrace it
It eluded my grasp
I thought it was certain
That I lived my life
With hopes and dreams
Of my childhood
But, Then
It became uncertain
I didn't know
What I was living?
Why I was living?
Where I was living?
The uncertainty
Devouring me
Gnawing at my flesh
Until there was nothing
Just a remnant
Of an uncertain life.

BORN TO LOSE

If there was a loser
Born to show the world
What a loser looks like
Then I am that person
To demonstrate a loser
For I was born to lose
In every aspect of my life
From great parents
To no parents
A promising career
To a desolate survival
I had it all
I lost it all
The world was mine
The world left me
I have no one to blame
But me
For it was me
Who made it happen
Ant it was me
That lost it all.

Career, loves, hopes, drams
The ashes strewn
All was my life
Occasionally sighting
A glitter in the ashes
I reach to touch
It scatters
As I chase the wind
To stop
So I can gather
What is left
In the dust
But it is too late
For I have forfeited
My destiny. Lost.

END TO END IT ALL

The end come to all of us
But what do we know of the end?
End of a life?
End of a soul?
End of a dream
That remained unfulfilled?
End to hopes
That keeps life alive?
Does the end even end
Or is it just a step
Of one end
That leads to the next end?
Does end even end
Or does it keep on going?
Then the end is not an end
Just the beginning of another end
As we hurl towards
Endless ends
Never encountering an end
Just ending
To start another
Just like life.

ROCKY RELATIONSHIPS WITH GOD

God and I don't get along.
I love Him; He loves me.
But we don't see
Eye to eye on many things.
I know His ways are deep
Too complicated for a simpleton life me,
But still I don't agree with Him
On many things.

He gave me great parents
But took them away
At a young age
Not cherishing their love.
I never got an answer
Why me?
I loved my parents.
I wanted them.
I needed them.
But I don't have them.

God give me a brain
A quest for knowledge
Desire to learn and grow
Creativity and idealism
And then gave me a mundane career
That favors materialism and survival.

God gave me ability to love
To feel passion
But then forces me
To live alone
Longing for companionship
That not only eludes me
But I may never find.

God gave me a personality
Charming with gentleness
To snatch the vision
When I stare in the mirror.

God gives me
The respect of values and integrity
To see my dreams shattered
By integrity and values.
God told me to be fair
To see unfairness thrive
I was told
Would catch-up with people, but
I don't see it.

Evil survives in glory.
Honesty is trampled.
Knowledge is squashed
To be replaced by mediocracy.

Yes, God and I
Don't see eye to eye.
I am not right, but
Nor is He.
But God is God.
I live with Him
In my heart.
I will forever,
But that does not mean
I agree with Him,
What He has done to me
For me
For His world
For His humankind
For rocky relationships
Will continue
Until eternity.

LIFE IS A PRISON

The day we are born
We are born in a prison
A prison called, "life"
It will enclose us
Until we die
What we do in this prison
Is up to us
Up to other prisoners
How we deal with them.
How they deal with us,
How they deal with you.

We search for a life
That is out there
Waiting for us
When we leave the prison
Which we will
In the end
But what awaits us
Out there
Is only in our imaginations
In our dreams.
But then, life is a prison.

A RELECTANT LIFE

I did not
Want to be born.
I did not ask for it.
Did I have a choice?
But I was born
So here I am
A reluctant human
Who lives life
But is not part of life.

I grew up reluctantly
To face the world
I did not want to face.
I reluctantly lived
An ambitious life
In a mediocre society
Trying to make a living
In a decaying society.

I did have dreams.
I did have hopes.
I did have faith
In myself.
But the world was consumed
By greed, self-interests
Materialism and consumerism.
Day-to-day existence
Fading into oblivion.

This is not the world
I dreamed of.
This is not the society
That I hoped for.
But I was born.
I had to live.

I chose to live
And hope to graciously
Pass into oblivion.
Just like the rest of humankind
But, reluctantly.

LIGHT AT THE END OF A TUNNEL

There is light
At the end of a tunnel
I don't know
I don't see
But it is there.
It has to be.
The tunnel is dark
But I am not lost
I know the way.
It is just
That I keep walking
In the dark
Hoping to see
A little light
To tell me
I am there.
But the emptiness
Continues to twist and turn.
I still can't see the light
Though I know
It is there.
It has to be.

ON MY BIRTHDAY

Every year
On my birthday
I reflect on the year
And every year
I come to the same conclusion
That it was a wasted year
Not much accomplished
Did my work
Survived
But nothing much
To show for it
Each year
I become a little more like the rest of humankind
Just existing
Going through the motions
Of mediocrity
And become me
I don't need
Birthdays to remind me of that
It is just another day
To remind me
Of the passing of a year.

ON AN ISLAND

I stand alone
On a small island
Surrounded by water
With no land in sight
Just water
Pounding the beach
Humans are no where
As I wait for a ship
To pass by
To see me
And take me,
But my island is my home.
It sustains me
I give it life.
We have learned
To live with each other,
Both lonely
And together.

THE ANIMAL IN US

There is an animal
In all of us
That becomes ferocious
When cornered
And threatened.
It lashes out
In full fury
Igniting passions
That seem
Untamable at the time.
Our mind is not our mind
It is possessed
By unseen forces
That dwell and mold it
Making us
Not what we are
A different person
That fails to
Recognize
The human in us
An envelops us
Consciousness
And all reasoning
Acting on
Primitive instinct
Of survival and threatened
To the point
That we are no longer
Humans
Of compassion and reasoning
Just a carcass
Of hate and bile.
It is horrible.
Something we must avoid,
At all costs.

For we are humans
We must be one
And act like one.
The animal in us
Needs to be vanquished
Gently and firmly
So we are not animals.
Human animals.

IF THE WORLD WERE NOT ROUND

I wonder
What would life be like
On Earth
If the world were not round
Just flat
With boundaries
That would limit us
And if we went
Beyond
We would fall into
The eerie universe
Lost forever
Among myriads of glories
Hurtling into unknown paces
Exploring experiences that would
Enlighten us
Unlike the round world
We live on
We go around in circles
Repeating history
Never learning from it.
Confusing East with West
For all directions are the same
If you go around in circles
Never finding a destination
Searching for humanity
That keeps us circling
Itself in confusion
Never finding peace
Always in turmoil with itself
That a flat world
Would not endure.
It is simple
With defined boundaries
A self-contained
World
With no exit.
I wish the world were not round.

I SAW MY LIFE IN A DREAM

It was a dream
Or was it reality?
Or is it still a dream?
I see my life before me
A beautiful life
Full of happiness and contentment
Home, family, a companion
Love effusing from every pore
It feels good
I am in a blissful state
And, then I wake up
I see myself
Just living and surviving
Lone and lonely
The dream was so beautiful
I want to live in it
I want the dream
To become a reality
But then dreams are dreams
Passing, fleeting memories
Of a live
That I want.

CULINARY SEXUALITY

Sex is life a food
One must eat it, enjoy it
Devour it with sensuous pleasure
Savoring every morsel
Its exquisite taste and smell
Using body and senses
In unison.
At the end,
We are satisfied.
We are full.
Time to rest.
Time to sleep
With fond memories.

FINDING LIFE

I was in the attic
Going through old boxes
That kept old memories
Of life
That I once lived
Beautiful and powerful
Events and happenings
That nurtured me
Shaped me
A product of the past
Bracing for the future
That hides my life
My aspirations, my dreams,
It is here sometimes
In one of these
Dust-covered boxes
That cover memories
That ignite passions
To find a life
That I lost
In the boxes
In the attic.

CRAWLING OUT OF A SHELL

I am surrounded
By darkness
Floating in a vacuum
Bracing myself
Against a thin membrane
That separates me
From light
I struggle
Pecking at the shell
Gently yet hard
Until I hear
A cracking sound
My pounding
Has created an opening
I see a glimmer of light
Inspiring my hope
As I shatter the shell
And crawl out
Brightness blinding me
As I venture into
An unknown wilderness
Accepting fate to guide me.

DYING WITH DIGNITY

Death comes to
All us mortals
As part of the life
That we are designed to lead
Culminating in a final moment
That transports us
To a different world
As we face the inevitable
The only thing that matters
Is that we die with dignity.
We do not know
How it will come.
We can never fully be prepared for it
Nut we can face it
With grace and charm.
And welcome it
As part of life
Embracing it
With love and affection
As it takes us
On a new journey.

MY OBITUARY

I search the papers
For my obituary
I just died
But not a mention
In any newspaper or magazine
My life could not be so wasteful
Not even a mention
Husband of so-and-so
Father of so-and-so
Just pages of emptiness
As I scan smaller prints
Searching for just a blurb
But nothing is there
I have just faded
Into oblivion
Memory to few
That will soon be forgotten
A price of an insignificant life
A life that no one knows
Even existed.

THE SCARET LETTER

My scarlet letter
Is stamped
On my forehead
A permanent mark
That I will carry
The rest if my life
The letter is "F"
It stands for "failure"
Everything I tried in life
Turned out to be a failure
My loves, relationships, careers,
Every step a failure
Failure of judgement
Failure of luck
Failure of timing
Failure of fate
Pride
It is a mark
I carry with pride
For I acknowledge it
I admit it
It is my destiny
A lesson of life.

THERE COMES A TIME

There comes a time
When one realizes
That one has done
As much as one can do
Tried what I had to
Some successes, some failures
Did the best
Under every circumstance
Time to accept
The results
And find
Peace
Within oneself
To prepare
For the inevitable
With peace and dignity.

THE EMOTIONAL VOLCANO

It erupts
With a force
Spewing ashes and debris
All over
Pent up emotions
Years of holding back
Hiding all these frustrations
Pummeled by the blows of life
Grinding into earth
With all the energy
Eager to unleash
The molten lava
The heat
Erupting into tears
To start the calming effect
As it cools down
To a dormant state
Below the surface
To stabilize the outside
Until the next eruption.

ALONE IN THE WILDERNESS

I stand alone
In the wilderness
Surrounded by tall trees
That hide
Any hint of my whereabouts
The flickering sunlight rays
Tell me that all directions
Are the same
I can venture into any direction
Not knowing where it will lead
As all paths are hidden
So I stand there
Alone and lonely
Protected by the trees
As the night comes
Trees whistle
And help me to sleep
I lay on the leaves
Hoping that the next day
Will show me the path
A path of new rays of the sun

ALONE IN THE DESERT

The sand is hot
Burnt by the scorching sun
I walk barefoot
Feet full of blisters
Searching for an oasis
That will give me
Shelter and water
The sand dunes taunt me
Gushing to blind me
I trad along
Hoping to see a mirage
That keeps me
Moving away from me
I run
I fall
The burning sand
Providing soft comfort
I crawl
Thirsty for life
The sandstorms shroud me
I flail with my hands
As the sand blasts me
With cruel blows
I tread along
In an unknown direction
Hoping for a miracle
The mind has hope
The body dwindling
The day shadows
Turn dark
The sand cools
I lie
Embracing its softness
Yielding to
A higher power
As I recoup my strength
For the journey
The next day may bring

I stare at the dark night
Waiting for one star
That will brighten to illuminate me
And give me a direction.
Fate.

THE LAST THROW OF THE DICE

I am standing
At an inviting gambling table
In a smoke-filled casino
Surrounded by eager players
Wishing for a fortune
That has eluded them
In real life
I have been gambling
A long time
Hoping that I will win some day
I win some
I lose some
Now, all I have left
Is enough for one last bet
Should I play it safe?
Or gamble it all
On one last throw
I win it all
On one last thrown
I win it all
Or I lose everything
It is my last hope
The last throw of the dice
My future rests on it
The deck awaits my decision
The players pass
Staring
While searching within myself
For the courage
To make a decision
Time is running out
And I must choose
I place my bet
I pick up the dice
My future is in my palm
I pray for Divine guidance
And let it go
The dice rolls

It sets
I stare at it
The numbers tell it all
My fate is decided
On the last throw
I move on
Life moves on

THE CIRCUS OF LIFE

Life is a circus
A show
To entertain the world
With acts of risk
Waiting for the applause
That comes when you succeed
A painful groan
When you fall
The artists
Trying death-defying
Feats
Soaring to new heights
Sometimes without a safety net
The audience applauding the risk
It is your life
The performer
Under constant gaze
As you soar and fall
Enjoying the thrill
Of life
That is nothing except a circus.

THE END IS NEAR

Life has to end some day
The day when
All scores are settled
We are one with ourselves
At peace and content
I can sense
The end
It is near
I can feel it
I can hear it
It's becoming
A gentle voice
That tells me
It is waiting
To hold me tenderly
It has been an exhausting journey
Over land and sea
And now I am tired
A place to rest
And move to a new world
The end is near.

THE FINAL PERFORMANCE

I stand on the stage
My last act
As the curtain falls
On my final performance
It was a great run
Full of life and some praise
The audience applauded
Sometimes standing cheers
How I say my last dialogue
I do it with passion
I have to leave
A lasting impression
A performance
That they will remember
All their life
I must do it
I put everything into it
Passion and soul
I am exhausted
It is over
The audience go hone
Another
The curtain falls
For the last time.

HUMAN HYPOCRISY

I am amazed
Each day
To discover
The extend of human hypocrisy
That says one thing
And does the opposite
We preach the
Value of human life
But have to question
Of buying guns
And killing other humans
Just for fun
We talk peace
But go to war
In the name of peace
We talk of love
Yet we cheat, rape and divorce
To satisfy our lust and ignorance
We learn and educate
To progress our illiteracy
We are
A hypocritic bunch.

BORN ON THE WRONG SIDE OF THE TRACK

I am traveling
On a train
Sitting alone in a lonely compartment
As the train thunders
Past hills and valleys
Bellowing dark smoke
That shrouds the skies briefly
I stare out the window
I see a parallel track
That races past me
Occasionally passing
Are other rumbling trains
Going in another direction
I wonder
Why I am on this train?
I belong on the other track
I boarded the wrong train
On the wrong track
On the wrong direction
What should I do?
I can't get off the train
I don't even know where I am
I don't even know where
I might end
Except that I am on the wrong track
The other track
Just reminds me
What I missed
I can only stare at it
But cannot be on it
I missed my town
I must complete my journey
Wherever it takes me
And bear the consequences
Of being on the wrong track.

THE DYNAMICS OF THE HEART

The heart is a strange creature
With a mind of its own
Ignoring where it resides
Throwing emotional tantrums
At whim
Falling in love
With anyone that it fancies
Ignoring the repercussions
Laughing at the brain
That it is so despairs
For the heart does not like logic
It is an emotional volcano
And then it hurts
It likes to see you in pain
It cries with joy
At your turmoil
It is satisfied
That it is in control
And teasing you
Until it has had its fill
And that is
The dynamics of the heart.

MY LIFE WITH ME

My life with me
Is at odds
Quite turbulent at times
We can't seem to agree
What is best for me.
It punishes me relentlessly
When I make mistakes
Even when I think
That life is unfair
We butt heads
On what direction to go.
Our paths diverge
We compromise
And wind up in a quagmire.
I blame life.
Life blames me.
The battle goes in.
It will end
When end coms
And life and me
Are not together.

BITS AND PIECES

I live my life
In bits and pieces
Some days I am happy
Some days I cry
Some days I wonder
Who am I?
Some days I feel lost
Some days I grope for me
But can't find myself
Some days I feel
I don't belong here
Some days I think
I am on top of the world
Some days I feel
I am at the bottom of the ocean
Each day
Brings a new set of challenges
Some exciting
Some troublesome
I handle them sporadically
Some with success
Some not
I endure mentally
Move forward
In spurts and gusts
Killing obstacles
Jumping over mountains
Dreaming of a life
That I may never have
Crashing violently
Against rocks of humanity
But I propel myself
Forward and backward
Living life
In bits and pieces
Just like most of us.

THE BROKEN ARROW

The arrow
That is ready
To propel forward
With all its might
To hit the target
It is intended for
To be broken
Wondering how
It will
Complete its purpose
It is ready at the bow
Drawn and pointed
But will it make it to its target
Or just fall to the earth
On its way
The string is let go
Broken
It must fly toward its target
Will it reach it?
Now, my hand of destiny
Will guide it
The broken arrow.

THE CURSE OF LIFE

I am cursed
The curse is my life
For it makes me live
A life that I do not want
It is not the life
That I dreamed of
It is not the life
That I was supposed to live
But I must live
At the cost of my life
To endure its pain and pressure
To drift across oceans and lands
In search of a place
That will give me
Peace and comfort
Where that is?
I do not know.
When will it happened?
I do not know.
I am cursed
And that is
My life.

THE FLICKERING FLAME

The flame
That burns in me
Is flickering
Emitting radiant colors
As it meets its destiny
Ready to extinguish
After illuminating
Most of my life
Lighting my way
So I could see
And not tumble
But ow the time is here
That it must extinguish itself
But before it sheds its light
It must flicker brilliantly
Radiating rainbow colors
To leave a legacy
That it still has fire
Within its heat
And wants to light up the world
One last time
Before eternal darkness.

THE PUPPET

I am a puppet
In this world
The invisible strings
Of life and fate guide me
I sing, I dance
I jump, I live
Each moment of my life
Is orchestrated
By the puppet master
Whose dexterous hands
Make me do things
That I find impossible
Some desirable, some undesirable
But I am just a puppet
With a happy face
To delight the world
With mu antics
Until the puppet master gets tired
And lets go of me
So I can rest in peace
Waiting futilely for the next dance.

NO LIFE IN LIFE

I have life
But there is no life
In my life
It is just life

That goes through
The daily motions of existence
To carve a living
In a stale world
That smells of mediocrity and decadence
While I try to
Put life in my life
Trying to breathe a fire
Into smoldering ashes
Where I see
The fire ebbing
Leading me
With just a life
That has lost
All luster
And is just
Cold as ashes.

THE FUTURE IS ENDING

I had a great future
I had great expectations
I dreamed about it
It was there
Within my grasp
I nearly touched it
Then it slipped
Out of my hands
I stared at an emptiness
The future just disappeared
One second it was there
The next second it left me
I keep holding
Empty space
Waiting for the future
To appear
So I can grasp it
And hold it tight
Before it leaves me
Grasping at the future.

BUILDING MONUMENTS OF ASHES

I grope through the ashes
Remnants of a life
That refused to live
Burnt to the ground
By cruel fate
And mental accidents
The ashes are rich
With love and memories
The only remaining remnants
Of human frailties
In a wayward world
I gather the ashes
Trying to protect them
From being blown away
By a sudden gust of wind
Scattering them on all paths
And people stop and step on them
I embrace them
Hold them in the palms of my hands
As I try to assemble them together
To erect a monument
That will tell
The story of my life
A life that was rich
In love, ambition and desire
I wanted to carve
Living statutes in mountains
Riding the waves
On turbulent oceans
Trek jungles
Where no light existed
To shine on the path
But Fate and Life
Never got along
Each step of life
Scarred the earth
Until all I had left
Were rich ashes

As I now gather them
To create a monument
To a life
That could be blown away
Any minute.

THE ABANDONED APARTMENT

It was beautiful
Overlooked a marketplace
Full of life and people
As goods were bought and sold
Elegant furniture
Beautiful ambiance
Effusing life
As time ticked on
The apartment became a burden
As each piece of furniture
Slowly vanished
Leaving a bare space
Empty and vacant
Desolate and cold
The sounds of the marketplace
Echo in empty rooms
Screaming for life
But it is over
For the abandoned apartment.

THE WAR WITHIN

Wars are brutal
Devasting human toil
But a war with oneself
Is even more brutal
For whom do you defeat?
The enemy is within you
You are your own enemy
No matter who wins
You lose
For the victory is temporary
As the turmoil
Will engulf you
And suffocate you
The dust will blind you
While you hope
That you will survive
But it is what's lost
What you have lost
You lost
The victory is an illusion
For eternal wars
Only end with you.

I AM JUST A SPECK

I am everything
I am nothing
As a minute speck
I am everything I need to be
I am one in a million
That exists
Without making a difference
As an individual
I am alive
As part of the universe
I am nobody
It is all
In the perspective
For a speck
I just a speck – nothing.

THE WISHING WELL

I stand at the rim
Of a wishing well
A dream that I never realized
Still hoping
That there is much more
In store for me
But what if my wish comes true?
Or my wish never comes true?
Will I gain or lose faith?
It is a risk
I must take
For what shall I lose
I have lost everything anyway
So I wish I could close my eyes
I toss the coin
I hear the hustle
And I open my eyes
And face the reality of my existence
Life goes on
Wishes or not.

BREAK THE SHELL

It is dark
I cannot see
I feel the walls
I can touch
I can sense
The air is stifling
I am out of breath
I have to get out
I have to break the shell
That I built for myself
To protect me
From the world
That enjoyed
Pounding me
The shell was
Comforting and warm
I was able to hide
Myself from me
Even my own air
Became stale
The world I erected
All of a sudden
Seemed alien
I could not recognize
My face in the mirror
It was dark
My breath was heavy
I pound on the wall
I have to break the shell
I need fresh air
I need sun
I need a new life
The shell cracks
I lean on it
I stick my head out
I breathe fresh air
I crawl out

I am free
To adventure
To new challenges
The whole world is mine
Now I am ready
To build a new shell.

LET THE ADVENTURE BEGIN

It has been
A boring life
The standard routine
Struggling for survival
The days pass
Uneventfully
Nothing to be proud of
It has no end
If I have to face
Myself in another life
I will say I did something
That made a difference
Life has been an adventure
A journey
That was entertaining and enjoyable
Challenges that challenged your brain
Full of risks and thrills
Otherwise we fade into oblivion
Erased from memory
I cannot let that happen
My life has to be an adventure
Let the adventure begin.

FAMILY OF ONE

When I was young
I had an idealistic vision
That when I grew up
I will have a family
Wife and children
Living in harmony
I did have a family
Wife and daughter
A storm came
That swept marriage away
I was left alone
Staring at the dust
With a daughter
Holding my hand
The passage of time
Turns my baby into a gorgeous woman
Ready for her life
To shape her world
The hand no longer holds mine
I stand alone
Staring at the sunset
A family of one.

THE CURSE OF LOVE

I have been cursed
By love
I want it
But can't find it
If I find it
I can't hold onto it
I try to extinguish
The feeling
But the more I try
 The more it awakens
It soars to heaven
And crashes me
Deep into the ocean
I can't swim
I can't sink
It just keeps me alive
Prodding and pricking
To make me move
But never finding peace
And that, to me,
Is the curse of love.

A PAINFUL SATIRE

My life story
Is a painful satire
Full of laughter
That makes you cry
Full of pain
That gives me peace.
Some occasional friends
Who constantly betray you
The permanent family
That treats you
Life an alien
I am surrounded by people
But I am alone
I try to reach and touch
But all I find is
An empty space
I want to hold love
But I get burnt by the flame
I try to run
But I stumble
Such is my life
A painful satire.

MY LIFE'S GROCERY LIST

If I were shopping for my life
What would I buy?
For breakfast
A cereal that will
Give me hope and strength
To face the day
Full of optimism and dreams
For lunch
The power
To propel me
To new worlds
To new worlds
That I could embrace
And love with my heart's desire
For dinner
The energy to rest in peace
Calm and tranquil
With a prayer of thanks
For snacks
To keep me on the right path
With dignity and courage
To face the next day
With hope.

I AM NOT GOOD FOR MYSELF

I was never
My favorite
I was never
Comfortable with me
Yet I tolerated myself
I had no choice
I was living with me
But I couldn't stand myself
So I fought and argued
With myself
At times I would win
But mostly I lost
The eternal struggle
The inner conflict
Just tore me apart
I lived a life
Devoid of life
Passing years
Just to pass time
As I lay my head down
In humility
Waiting for the final sleep.

PATTERN OF BEHAVIOR

I have a pattern
Of behavior
That is self-destructive
I dream of a life
That I should like to live
But I crush those dreams
By cutting the foundation
Until the entire structure collapses
I dream of love
That would elevate me
To the bosom of heaven
And then I sabotage it
With my ignorance of reality
I dream of faith
In myself and my abilities
And then I embark on a path
That tramples my values
And I sit on scattered dust
I look in the mirror
And only see the person
That I wanted to be
I have alienated myself
With the pattern of my behavior.

WASTED BRILLIANCE

I was brilliant once
That is what I thought
But it was an illusion
The flashing light
The brief glitter of brilliance
Before it extinguishes
Into rays of hope
Searching for a dream
That remains a mirage
I can think it
I can find it
But it always hides from me
I could blink
And figure it out
What it was all about
I could connect the dots
Of life and existence
But now I search
For the next dot
That eludes me
And makes me wonder
Wishing life was brilliance.

ABOUT THE AUTHOR

Dan Khanna considers himself a traveler through life enjoying an adventurous journey. Dan was born in New Delhi, India. After he completed high school, at St. Columbus High School, Dan left India striking out for California via short stays in London, Montreal and Milwaukee, Wisconsin. Although his dream was to pursue a career in the arts, acting, music, and writing, a quirk of fate placed him in engineering college and pursuing a business management career, in which he excelled. Dan completed an undergraduate program in engineering, and a Master and Doctorate in Business Administration.

Dan worked in Silicon Valley's high technology firms and was a CEO and founder of several firms. He changed careers to be a professor. Now, he again is pursuing his dream in creative endeavors.

Dan is the quintessential Renaissance Man, whose interests span the gamut of the arts, sciences, history, social and political studies, classics and philosophy. His search for knowledge began in his early life where his father was the Chief Education Officer of Delhi and his mother was a Sanskrit scholar. Dan speaks English, Hindi, Urdu, Punjabi, and Gujarati.

As a child, Dan read voraciously, particularly enjoying novels, such as Sherlock Holmes, Agatha Christie, Earl Stanley Gardener, Ian Fleming's James Bond series and classic works of Shakespeare, Tolstoy, Dickens, Oscar Wilde, Thomas Hardy, and other writers. He was very interested in poetry and read English poems of Browning, Keats, Milton, Tennyson, and Frost, as well as, other poets, while mastering Urdu poetry. His intellectual interests including studying Western and Eastern philosophers, especially Socrates, from whom he learned questioning methodology employed in his research, lectures and seminars.

During his parochial education, Dan was interested in various sports: cricket, soccer and field hockey. His love for the arts and music was honed to a level that he performed in plays, movies and solo concerts.

Dan's present journey is devoted to creative arts and activities, primarily writing poetry, fiction and non-fiction books and plays, while continuing to acquire knowledge of diverse subjects. He has published one book and has written over twelve hundred poems. Dan has several non-fiction and fiction books in development.

www.ingramcontent.com/pod-product-compliance
Lightning Source LLC
Chambersburg PA
CBHW071301040426
42444CB00009B/1824

HAPPY CLOUD MEDIA LLC PRESENTS:

EXPLOITATION NATION

DOWN THE RABBIT HOLE	2
NON-MAMMALS ATTACK!	5
DAY OF THE ANIMALS (1977)	11
PIGS 'N CROCS	14
GRAPHIC WORM HORROR!	23
CROCODILE (1980)	31
QUARANTINE 2020: DOUBLE FEATURE	33
MANEATING MOTIFS: THE LONGEVITY OF SHARK ATTACK 3: MEGALODON	38
ROAR: WHEN ANIMALS ATTACK FILMMAKERS	43
GRIZZLY II: REVENGE	46
I WAS KILLED BY A 6-FOOT SCORPION	48
WELL, I WONDER, WONDER WHO...WHO WROTE THE BOOK OF THE DEAD? OH, RIGHT...TOM SULLIVAN	38
TOM SULLIVAN IN SPLATTER MOVIE	60
IN THE MOUTH OF MADNESS	63
STUART GORDON: MAESTRO OF MONSTERS	71
STUART GORDON: ARTAUD FOR ARTAUD'S SAKE	77
TOM SULLIVAN SIDEBAR ON WARP!	83
NO RESPECT. NO RETURN. NO RESISTANCE.	86
TAMMY, TANNY, SOMEONE'S IN LOVE	95
WHAT OUR FRIENDS ARE UP TO	99
I'D BUY THAT FOR A DOLLAR!	103
Back issue pages like REAL magazines used to have!	109

Exploitation Nation is published by Happy Cloud Media, LLC.
Vol. 1, No. 9 © 2020

Amy Lynn Best:
Publisher
Mike Watt:
Editor
Carolyn Haushalter:
Asst. Editor
Ally Melling:
Copy Editor

Contributors:
**Bill Adcock
Dr. Rhonda Baughman
Pete Chiarella
Jason Paul Collum
Mike Haushalter
Shawn Jones
Jason Lane
Ross Snyder
Douglas Waltz
Justin Wingenfeld**

Cover Art:
Tom Sullivan

Art Direction and Layout:
Ryan Hose

Special Thanks to:
**John Walter Szpunar
Pat Reese
Andy Rausch
Tim Thomson
Holt Boggs
Honey Lauren
Justin Channell**

All photographic and artistic content copyright the original holders and is included here for promotional purposes only. No rights are implicit or implied.

Exploitation Nation is published periodically by Happy Cloud Media, LLC (Amy Lynn Best and Mike Watt, PO Box 216, Venetia, PA 15217). Exploitation Nation Issue #9 (ISBN 978-1-951036-19-5) is copyright 2020 by Happy Cloud Media, LLC. All rights reserved. All featured articles and illustrations are copyright 2020 by their respective writers and artists. Reproductions of any material in whole or in part without its creator's written permission is strictly forbidden. Exploitation Nation accepts no responsibility for unsolicited manuscripts, DVDs, stills, art, or any other materials. Contributions are accepted on an invitational basis only. **Visit us at Facebook.com/ExploitationNation and www.happycloudpublishing.com**

DOWN THE RABBIT HOLE

When the COVID-19 virus hit, we all understood that we'd have to make sacrifices both small and large in order to combat the pandemic. In typical Neanderthal fashion, many of us sank to the occasion and decided that any sacrifice was tyranny. A lot of those folks are dead now.

The biggest loss we at Happy Cloud suffered was the cancellation of April's Cinema Wasteland Movie and Memorabilia Show. Most of our readers are Wastelanders. It's a twice-a-year show held in Strongsville, Ohio, and owned and operated by our friends and family, Ken and Pam Kish. Because of this show, I am personally guaranteed eight days of happiness per year. Because of the pandemic, I am down four.

In some respects, it's silly to see this as a loss. The cancellation kept my Wasteland family safe. It's a small thing compared to how so many wound up unemployed, ill, lost, and depressed. The Kishes made the right call, as did the Holiday Inn that hosts us. But with all the quarantine, it's easy to lose sight of the "us" and focus solely on the "I." Even the best of us are susceptible to self-pity.

Still, while I love horror conventions, Wasteland is something special. We've been attending since 2002 and have held a prime spot at the front of the room, right between Ken and Pam and our side-family, *Ultra Violent Magazine*. (*EN* and *UV* share many creative elements and staff.) It's one of those increasingly rare low-impact shows. It doesn't tease attendees with photo ops, tiered ticket pricing, or long lines to see expensive celebrities. (I still can't get over seeing a price tag of over $100 to meet Rob Schneider at Chiller. That's more than he's paid to make movies!) What it offers is all WYSIWYG

face value: DVDS, books, toys, handcrafted items, and pop culture icons who hang with you in the restaurant after hours.

For me, Wasteland is equal parts unpretentious swap meet and intellectual salon. I've had April conversations interrupted by a six-month hiatus, only to pick up where we left off in October. I've imbibed with people from all walks of life, and Wasteland welcomes everybody. The only rule is to not be a dick. You can easily find others who dig what you dig and aren't going to ding you if they don't.

We can get rowdy. Being close to the airport, the hotel hosts pilots and crew, and sometimes they look askance at us poor revelers. We've had run-ins with wedding parties as well. (One poor bridesmaid got freaked out by one of our regulars dressed as an evil clown. He chased her around attempting to apologize, to make sure she knew he wasn't a party of her phobia. One of our more sensitive staff, Reign, thenchased after *him*, imploring, "You're making it worse!") But for the most part, outsiders end up joining us. Again, all are welcome. We have ex-Nazis, as well as a lot of career criminals, bikers, folks in recovery, and folks failing recovery. But it's all a release. It's difficult to be anxious at Wasteland. Nobody is judging you. We're all there for the singular reason: to escape the horrors of the outside world by wrapping ourselves in the protective huddle of friends we only see twice a year.

Thanks to Wasteland, I've had breakfast with multiple Leatherfaces. We physically dragged Jimmy Lorinz (*Frankenhooker*) across the restaurant to join us for dinner. Many of those

Some of our Wasteland Family: L-R: (?), copy editor Ally Melling, Andy Dixon, Mike and Carri Natarelli, editors Mike Watt and Amy Lynn Best (center), Jill and Greg of LIX, Brian Huey, Sofia, art director Ryan Hose, artist Colin Rogers, U/V editor Art Ettinger. (Photographer as yet unknown. All Rights Reserved)

3

working on this mag were trapped in the dodgy Left-Side elevator with Dee Wallace (who did *not* appreciate our cannibalism jokes or when Jason Lane called the front desk: "Hey, uh, we're trapped in your elevator and— Hello?").

One year, we were hanging in the lobby. It was about 2 in the morning, and a random group of elderly bagpipers in kilts wandered in, played "Amazing Grace," and fucked off again. Another year, we were in Sid Haig's room when a tornado touched down nearby and caused a blackout. It didn't stop the party. Then, the bar decided to stop serving alcohol. That's when people went feral. By 4 a.m., we were still out in the hallways. Someone at the rear of the corridor screamed at us to shut the fuck up! Our outrage fizzled instantly when we realized what time it was and how we were affecting those not of our circle. So, the fuck up we did shut.

One year, someone had set up a beer pong table right outside our door. All night we heard, "YEAH!" "SHHHH!" "...*Yeah*."

It's hard to be mad about that.

Sequestered inside for months on end, I've been in touch with my fellow Wastelanders via Facebook and the various meeting apps, but it isn't the same. I'm holding my breath for October. Outside, there are protests and riots, violence and prayer circles. Our so-called leaders are fomenting violence against their own people. Meanwhile, COVID-19 continues to tear through the world.

Come October, I'll need Wasteland more than ever.

U/V Editor and Deep Red scribe Art Ettinger with yours truly. This is a good depiction of our relationship.